W9-AAN-340

voodoo hypothesis

VOODOO

hypothesis

poems

CANISIA
LUBRIN

A Buckrider Book

© CANISIA LUBRIN, 2017

No part of this publication may be reproduced, stored in a retrieval
system or transmitted, in any form or by any means, without the prior
written consent of the publisher or a license from the Canadian Copyright
Licensing Agency (Access Copyright). For an Access Copyright license,
visit www.accesscopyright.ca or call toll free to 1-800-893-5777.

Buckrider Books is an imprint of Wolsak and Wynn Publishers.

Cover and interior design: Natalie Olsen, Kisscut Design
Cover photograph: lomomiket / photocase.com
Author photograph: Anna Keenan
Typeset in Surveyor
Printed by Coach House Printing Company Toronto, Canada

 Canada Council **Conseil des Arts**
for the Arts du Canada

 Canadian Patrimoine
Heritage canadien

ONTARIO ARTS COUNCIL
CONSEIL DES ARTS DE L'ONTARIO
an Ontario government agency
un organisme du gouvernement de l'Ontario

The publisher gratefully acknowledges the support of the Canada Council for the
Arts, the Ontario Arts Council and the Government of Canada.

Buckrider Books
280 James Street North
Hamilton, Ontario
Canada L8R 2L3

Library and Archives Canada Cataloguing in Publication

Lubrin, Canisia, 1984–, author
Voodoo hypothesis / Canisia Lubrin.

Poems.
ISBN 978-1-928088-42-4 (softcover)

I. Title.

PS8623.U215V66 2017   c811'.6   c2017-904866-X

CONTENTS

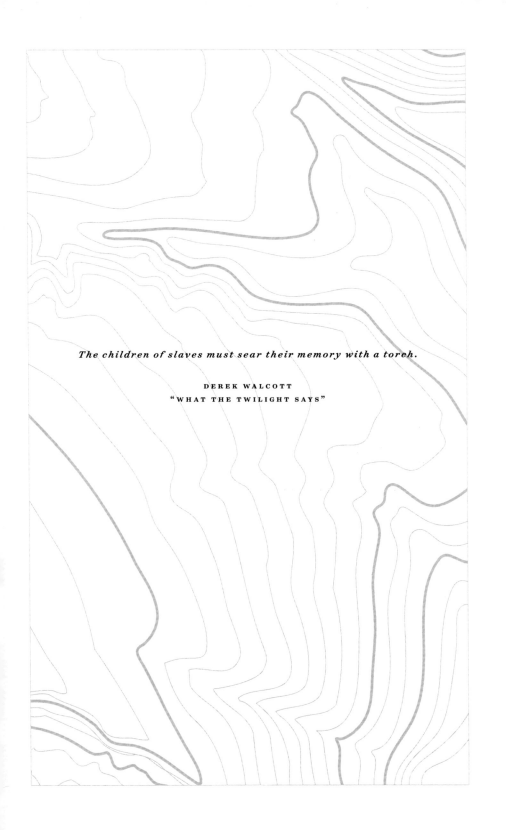

The children of slaves must sear their memory with a torch.

DEREK WALCOTT
"WHAT THE TWILIGHT SAYS"

VOODOO HYPOTHESIS

Before sight, we imagine
that while they go out in search
of God
we stay in and become god,
become: Curiosity,
whose soul is a nuclear battery
because she'll pulverize Martian rock
and test for organic molecules
in her lab within a lab within
a lab. She doesn't need to know our fears
so far too grand for ontology, reckoning.

Did you not land with your rocket behind
you, hope beyond hope on the tip of your rope
with the kindness of antigravity slowing you down,
you, before me, metal and earthen. But I am here to
confirm or deny, the millions of small
things that seven minutes of success were hinged upon
when I was little more than idea and research,
in the hypnotic gestures of flame and Bunsen burner,
and into parachute
no one foresaw, the bag of rags at the end
of the tunnel – all memory now,
this Paraclete.

Where else is a pocket
of air more deadly than the atomic bomb?
Would this only happen on Earth?
Has Mars run out of tolerance for the minutiae

of air pockets, fingerprints and worry?
Aggregates of metal, Curiosity
and her clues to calm our fears for what's coming.
Mars and her epic storms, her gargantuan
volcanoes have long ceased their trembling,
her crazy flooded planes, frozen and in cinema.
Martian life now earth and revelation's phases:
Earth problem, not Mars problem.

But why
should I unravel over all this remembering?
     Great thing about landing
     is that I've arrived

at your service, at your sand, at your valley
and unsentimental magma.
Before me screams planes like Mojave Desert, Waikiki, Nagasaki,
nothing too strange to keep Curiosity off course.
Even though the Viking missions found no conclusive pulse
and we declared you dead, O Mars,
never mind that we named your heights and depths
from orbit. And from your spheres of minerals
where oceans once roared – we've learned little
of your lenience for empire.
Forgive us what Spirit uncovered in the silica of your ancient hot springs.

Ah, yes, we've come back home.
Phoenix told us we inherited the numberless
stories of your hydraulic pathologies
but I am Curiosity. If I kill the bitch right,
she'll take us deeper and convince us to send earthlings
to set up Earth colonies on your deserts. They won't ever
come back, but that's not so bad when we trade in
the grander scheme.
As though the colonials, the Tribe Traders
and all the pharaonic masquerades of gone times
were not fair threat. That we won't know the depth
of our homeward seas
is nothing when

the sun's still got our backs.
And while waters still vaporize before us
Curiosity will keep on until the organic secrets
of that Martian puzzle become as household to us
as carbon. Oxygen wasn't the only disaster to befall Earth,
to bless her with life.

Apollo drilled on the moon and got stuck
and the harder we've drilled down here
the more we've loosened our screws.
Perhaps there'll be no one left to give
a damn about the death of our privates

unless we prove ourselves enigmas,
the alien we think we know is the alien we only dream
up starting from the bottom
of the Curious.

We wake and die through
the crowns and thorns and craned chapters,
we move too quick for understanding.
Still, through the decades we predict,
Curiosity confirms the cold-slain dust.

Then come her conches blown
in the hard-won postcards travelling
on space dust faster than a bullet
to say:

hey,
I'm here. I safe. Wish you were here.
See Gale Crater, Mount Sharp, just as you've said.
Come bask with me in the wonders of a Martian. Good afternoon,
you of flowering faith. Set sail for home,
because we will all wear the consequences of this choice.
And you never should have said
goodbye.

THE MONGREL

There was no name for us in our mother's oratory.
– SAINT-JOHN PERSE

√

Still unravelling from ghosting stars,
she moves us, light-formed, cue,
of Mongrel, also a corpse, but of steel,
curved, down earth's scrubbed sands,
on a single gust of wind,
and her body through a doorway,
she shrinks hundredfold,
to size of Earth: moments ago, forgotten,
now dreamt Mongrel: a fur city, no more
archival than ancient than still warm and
she'd done nothing except bawl *the lost,*
are enough! The science, inexact like birth
is Mother, Mongrel alive in the street-chained light –

≅

If from above, the Mongrel's Creole maps
mathless, a late-life scar that carts its wounded
head on the surface of a jaundiced stream, she – feral
with remembrance, her black-rock heart must hide
pressure-cooked islands, stormed space where
Einstein's quadrate bones scurry to mount Nèg maron.
      Slave-hand revolts at the green mouth of Hades:
      how Mongrel rites wrap fur against a Native
      is address to Caliban, the animal that knew it had been
brutalized by men. But fine. By now, the seas are vague,
and even the exploded Carina spares us, wanderlust
and relative need for lightspeed, systems and fall-off –

≠

There is blood, seldom ache, where the avail-
able light reaches down past levels of dog,
cow's grass, tribe, pitch and burn, the wild
brutality loves us this side of the name, while
only misted, our ears stretch to still the Mongreled
air landing, broken, invented again as *history*
        in the rusted coils of coffee shops, inked
Mongrel skins, whose only escape is one cosmic
blue carbuncle. What is the right way to sway
the Black bruising self, elegant as a question
mark can curve into harp and vein and matter,
dark with blows like from God, cannibal and castoff –

≥

The Mongrel was still breaking, offing,
in a pale blue nutshell of monk's milk and tar
when life exposed the carapace of her skull.
Bit, where ancestors drew their roots up
those walls of knotted blood, on a throne
that names a million years into entering an illusion
        of singed bamboo, then ships
come and night comes and stays and soon
these generations miss their gills, scales
and talons, still dug into old valleys, still
lulled by disappearing suns, by broke hours
of bone branding flesh, held dark through
immortal dark, a gleam of that riverine name –

≤

Inside the wounded name, she gathers like dust
down the corduroy route, the Mongrel
heart in her hand – once part of a waist-high
Earth, then life upward started with the trees and
untroubled by the termites, still one hundred
million years off and withered on the brow of chance.
Together, they disappear to plot with the cliffs
    from which will protrude pavement
and aperture, time: a Mongrel's walk to the place of these pines.
Collapse, then, into leather boot and this smoked hunger and re-enter
the story: that Nova Scotia beach aglow with Mongrel flame –

∞

Now if she knew to sit, downed by the blunt breath
of doubt, would she have troubled the Mongrel
with music and milk and names and trenches,
those miles so deep? What else reveals us, a species
of amnesiacs, cut off from the trembling that tore –
our continents apart? And with so much unknowing
like this view, like rising smoke reveals the Eden
continent, preserved in the blind spot of a pictured
confession: this grief, a story with swords and bite, sun
whose silence holds the invisible pulls of distant worlds, wars
unhinged from the shoulder blades of gods. The Mongrel's
orienting grace is still its tail, showing up for things to come,
signalling that our knowledge of the Mongrel is only fragmentary –

AFTERSHOCKS
for Dionne Brand

No rescue. Escape was
the farthest she could come,
away from that island – that chance
she would take on that stone
in her hand, on a place
with no one she knew.
Perhaps the signs were all
reflex, the habit of aftershocks
bare in a new world she leavens.

A world that could not
last without the lye of her.
Bloodlines, anyplace
recalled, memory had etched
the tunnels of, a nameful hundred
rivers gulling the roads, before
. the miracle of driftwood,
malls and factories, the greying
walls of rooms cramped with all
familiar, the ranking plumes that vanish –

leaving us curled.
What we long for
is hard to explain.

   Like false pentameters
Credo on our Cupid's bow
of wild continent, naming
another place that sees
the barren clearing claimed
and loved. What psalm spends
its many selves in code
or water, vernacular and captive
        leaves her new century
relic: by another life made up
enough to strike star-music
against the weight of her island,

like the sampled
high-pitched moan of the dodo
as it falls into that chasm of loss.

Linger, my sandmaker breath,
slap up against the walls of this house.
        Fill up here
in the city or two-thirds out
at a distance's abrupt portrait
things for which learned names would not do.

And what have I? Have I forgotten too

what that thick slab of noise
drowns and drowns beneath
her age? That passage
for the persisting flesh already locked
and knocking in its burned metal slip.

Now begins the singe of winter
against the spring with its penitence
of altered meaning. And now
the birds are not the little things with tunes
about the horror of mountains.
Linger: ocean, voodoo sea
        ending with morning.

Now hold – with whatever is left,
whatever trembles with a noise
nobody but the radiator makes,

no usual sound of crickets, frogs
    and chorus of beetle –
            the cry of whatever now lives
            alone with the matchbox's
            crude apostrophe, mantle and heat
            on her wreath, birthing new worlds
            at the great road's hush.

    There rots a rescue –
rescue is too much to ask
        of anywhere –

OUR MAPLESS SEASON

I too am redacted, unsuitable reptilian,

      shell of speech I have forgotten,
      unless ravines can drown
each sound they cup from my throat.

Exposed against this anemone August
      is a way of unlearning
leeching questions, what mischief starves in *whys*.

Why – because too much is the way
      of knowing the chrysalis before
it crumples in the sun.

Mud-formed mirror of this sea-formed
   rotunda reminds too much
of this face and will, like my mother's

elusive redraft, blood-knot
in the spilling
generations' menses –

what must have started some sweet day
we can only feign to rescue
      from the old Carib cleanse
by test tube and accelerants,
      in empire's wildfire ditched in our bays.

These are the many ways of love,
learned in the book's
dye of our distrusts,
fighting these combustive,
Antillean understandings of *why*.

The still-revolt of our bones' sacred tow –
unmixable light
   measured in the hummingbird's mapless hum,
scattering this day, only just up,
deep into the ground.

Why, even with twelve litany of litanies
or reasons to stop
    would they choose you
            and sell you
            and stamp you
            and keep you – brief
            and name you
            and slit you down to kin
            and name you
            and call you
            and breed you, bar you
            and breed you, room you
            and jail you, jail you and cage you, cage you and cage you

KEEPERS OF PARADISE

This is a hand that intends to do its maker harm.
This is the clock turned back five hundred years.
        The river that runs from Eden mouth
        to rare unsweetened mouth.

I've logged the sour dawns of all
my quiet into this body,
its crisis of fleeing nowhere when nowhere is home.

And reborn half-bled in our nighttime
diverging their sullen brethren, their patterns of vapour,
rain, shadows on goat-eaten planes
in the Morse events of smallest things –
in my new metropolis away.

I am a simple child, then, a tilled site of history.
Call me isobar. Distraction in place of earth.
Call me tropical depression

        where I regale to the world its problem of beaten pines,
pleading rivers returning thorns to their abducted bush.
I'd offer the wound night shuts behind my eyes –

But enough. Hear Morne D'or divinize her song.
        Give these coon keepers of paradise a liminal eavesdrop.
Hear ghostly algorithms translate these nights to bloom.

CHILDREN OF THE ARCHIPELAGO

*For us in the archipelago the tribal memory is salted with the
bitter memory of migration.*
– DEREK WALCOTT, "THE MUSE OF HISTORY"

Nursed out of miracles and half-sunken
in an island house that schools
uneven mercies, closure's soft states
the morning after the unflawed acoustics of the tomb
have been silenced.

You would think we'd all gathered here
for the chasing of childhood friends,
to learn again the primal dance
of our bodies on pom d'amou trees like the souring
lessons of staying meek,
      or at least to sample the business of such prophecies'
      rumoured rhizome of sun streaked on horizon.
What bittersweet voodoo

we revive: dreams we walked down school hallways,
music we shackled to the streets en mas,
costumes now wary between us
and the wrecked bacchanal, all
less familiar than silversmiths'
work ornamenting
        our necks. Something slipped by current
        from the Nile welcomes us back. Our foreign dollars
        stretching the tongue – big-time Mongrelian road twisted
        to re-walk mizi maladi. We roil to re-remember.
        This world – even at its most toutouni.

Mama, whatever we collapse here
and bind up in grey matter, let it be
our own in another life, where
the magic of selling nothing could hold
glass in our spine and bread in our mouth,
     transubstances of all our doubt inviting
the universe's mothered
          things. Like what is born and has died
in its desire of the world, what we'd shout from
galvanized rooftops, what we'd label dread
like sapien-luck.
          Then one morning let us find our nakedness again,
in that pure sun of our dry season, where some great beast,
some malfini stacking leaves in our names
could make us spell the might of the Sahara,
or the seaward inchoate in our iris' dents.

Without thirst or grief or figment
in the straight Creole
namesake: malfini – wrong end.
     But we find the balsam of the meek's green lot tempting
as the place we left in waiting. It has stopped noticing
our absence, of course. Our absence, still the point.

A place on stolen land to lay our heads as our parents
pray our bad chance away
in the coalpot buttressed by the father who hugs his son
and cries the Atlantic into his nape
the mother who holds her daughter
and drinks the Atlantic from her nape
ten years pass before they have seen
the ones they have not since
appearing as some evergreen law.

So we return to bury or burn what is left of our departed,
whose last great epitaphs cloud all evidence of skin.
And what's in a name but the pirated
exhausts of our departure.

Such will, darlin' archipelago. What cage, our own
small frames gather in the vast burden of mortality.
      Be poised then, however our shadows play
our address still on the vivarium
slipped disks of everywhere:
      on the market-frail urgency of street
bulb, canoe and fire,
      tempest and privilege in the work
of lightning – epiphanic
      these savage hymns of thunder consoling
any blessing to mud.

What hurricane out there, crazed Caribbean,
centuries old, still framing our manners
  for a plaintive four hundred years,
  swallowing things many times the size of our earth,
     still a grief at ease – at least,
this hard precipitous thing, it is ours.
      Nothing we have mastered
still keeps our mourning ours.

Remember hanging, remember the centrifuge of hammock
and the whole life held up by one nail. Remember the haunt-bound
          hoards of cane, the sun-strip banana fields
          that set us out for tenements
          that could not love us broken or whole.

          Remember our bruises hid in looping dwòl English.

          We bear them, though not enough to undream

our seabed trail of islands – unbrittle homes ransacked
in cannibal froths of sea.

          We, game – the hour before children
          rote and oxidized believers – the hour after.

THE FRANKENSTEIN UNIVERSE

Like the canary – testing the depths
of the black before cave, before light

and speed broke new wounds
– I can't tell you there won't be

any towers to climb the heart
that won't tick, the toe that has forgotten

how to balance the body that has had its organs
auctioned at the price of an ashen brown leaf

I can't tell you how maps the trail retouched
with the hushed tune of the denigrate

or that instrument carving time out
of where was nothing. I can't tell

you where was born the N-word.
If upturned from a tender history,

if bent first of a semaphore absence
of jail bars and voodoo dolls – out

from which the cartographers came,
stood and looked up at the lipped beauty of a half moon

and christened star, iris, too. And like one Columbus
pupil 'membering an early death quickened like a lie,

made earth of pencils' brittle ends.
Drew bedtimes or beasts hidden in a fort –

chanting down the snow where speeding angels leap
too high for the dark girls' rumours

of release, ochre's in a green flash of sky.
So wait for the big thing to tell us

today is a good day to dream, it doesn't matter if it rains,
if we were all returned to nondescript

matter, if we speak equations of hardness into the human,
if forests mime limbs that never loped through the hickory, lime and oak

like dogs strapped and able to mourn us. What is it like if day
floods the boughs closed to the high life, if lesser valves filled

with sea grit opened at the dawn of flesh
through to what birthed the BBQ.

But take it all at once: do splitting cells not prove bodies that glide
in slipstreams of molasses are also once and for all at home?

If proof is what you seek: these doors, clear with fright
and conscience burst at the hinges and turn out all ill this life deposits,

however cosmic the unease, into the black sweater
of nighttime. I can't tell you what marks the hills that wait

like hexagrams of frost. But behold the sweet, holy reprieve
of a hoodie pulled over the eyes in wanton praise

of the pre-bang dark when the world is too much.
Instead the sun comes up announcing it has touched the parts of us that hurt,

the parts we swath in children's clothes, that name
the armfuls of us still earthbound. Still logged in cities that perch

in our chests like windows into our own green galaxy.
Far out, though, spirals keep close and unchanged the coordinates

of our birth,
who else remember how they force our dismember?

THE STATIONS OF THE CROSS

                                    Homing into a self
in the mud here whose vision edges teeth – we arrive late and upright.
Some satellite of loosened scriptures

anchoring our stories where the drowned look back at Columbus's
bended knee, weep still, one-third buried, our heads in the virgin woods:

where all of earth's water boils down to a drop – mothers demand
I speak though I cannot speak, children,

       whole as my favour transfigured by roads,
       rag dolls disappeared from one hallowed tomb.

       A walk for five days in flicker of lamps
       to sample them, the Stations of the Cross.

       Ebbed
       like lit lesions in the table, we arrive
       like last season's revived fruits.
       Still we are midnight, first light
       and everything I gleam is decimated folk,
       taxing endless renewals
       in the mastering of my mother's creole bread.

       My hand fears its own speech of lines.
       They fault with every backward swing through time.

       A boundless love for the cutlass
       my mother has dug into
       the patron earth to keep our meals far
       from the lonely atrophy of a watered bowl.
       So we wash our feet with myrrh squeezed
       from the lips of fatigued, blue-lacquered children
       only one hour awake and impartial
       to the crowing cock.

       Who prolongs that ruined arm pointing
       clear the day?

Mothers the tan path forgive their varicose-proof
of affliction. Fathers downed even from miles out
chanting *fruitless what we do*. Sisters invited and vanished,
sages bearing the extinction of some degraded arrival,
arranged for escort. The upright can still petition
the moss to lay humbly its sober greening.

Blessed they who hear all and nothing but the canticle
of this place.
Mountain streams birthing rivers to hold our unknowable
gone, believed indexed in the geography of our cleft cups.

Now we keep every broken thing at our table,
where we roll and ignite the Old World's plea for innocence,
take and swallow the troubled incense.

But never mind what we eat, what portraits the naked
bowl with more thirds of our lives marooned from
a crevice of ground
ripe in us, what is hard to possess,
    like God-speech
    but loosened,

how we ferry this earth, by such strange cyclic chemistry –
all of our fruitless pieces swaddled
in the gaped rays of some Easter sun.

BASTIAN PLANE

The spectral family ends in
landscape or something close
to battleships conjoined, close
to mechanics of scale: minus ports, desperate
in its possibility, as always to map such unions
ousting marriage with wars

> Them knights patrol on dogback
> clash with fourteen-times coast,
> fourteen wars I never archer

> > Still, if my need come down
> > from good talk, from bright abrading
> > ribbons in the stratosphere

> the land, the house on meadow
> without the bruised foundation
> of them white towers and kings

> you'll flag their heartbeat in my own.

> Open the window if you need
> > to scream,

if you must set the fleets
back now to tax – we, lightening gods,
my mother and history, slipped
like bad Toledo sugar into tea and sea
risen to cloud.

Now   we
sands   battered   apart by storm
     rage   by
     still

     water   and search
                                for we

reflection

          in the dark

NOWHERE THE PYTHAGORAS

falters against
does the light
carrying its divisible things
less delicate than the blackening
flames that chaperone each dawn
into whips, lash me as I think today
to press down harder into some
sacrifice of numbers, dream
and song.

The implanted celestial I had
dreamt is that same high dream
of disembodied legs quickening
to the ivory sands of the coast.

> I'm hurt, you know, that call
> to end the trouble by,
> by which I mean no longer
> the self, which is the right way to
> crook
> the wild I stuff too easily
> into

> this abandoned gospel left
> to these daughters, saving the
> imperceptible savannah,
> setting off arrows that fall at right
> angles

on the tan woollen path,
in the hoarded field,
in one matted clump
maybe empire is fallen, is scattered as the dew,

but trouble – and there is no blade wearier
than this, how we speed through it, glacially,
like things the Lord sayeth,
rightfully restoring the damp to its parched ground,
this trouble I plot against you where small fires tongue-lash
my dark, dark pulse, is still original, still not for me

Measure this: wicked looks like glass and is blind.

GIVE US FIRE OR THE BLACK PROMETHEUS

We saw no need to keep
on our intoxicating cocoons,
to show our best parts
swallowing the sun. Miss me
with that predecessory sort
of exorcise. Or magic-like
teething skin in the black guts
of slave ships, we're through with being

you, or that Ulysses figure: let us squall
with old Prometheus any day. See his thin tribal
mask, his dangling sun-sprout earrings,
watch him fete with ancient pan-Africa
when light was first a spectre cassava root
between three Nubian twigs,
a banished dawn,
millennia before the powers of Europe echoed
those flames in the chambered defaults
that buried him –

In the faux conduits of barely recalled sex
nongenders raised sorceries
and some unsought vocabulary past what
it means to say any conscious thing, like
folks, we all lost to the flat-stoned riots
of history's masters and Titans. Split and erect.

What of Papa Bwa? See his straw hat,
gaped Rasta smile in a shanty near the bay,
freckled from weaving dried palms into vision
of world peace, vision of God – what falls from
these burning hills. What parallels
pull apart to make the self unsolvable?

From these elisions of a half-life flicked off,
the world hardens like fat crusted in the eyes
on a cold mid-morning. She'll never know she
held something cursive, x'd in the tremble of her

wrists, both hands skilled
to anchor against them, reverb of net zero,
reverb of bitumen, that near-Biblical spill of liquid dawn
and the flames she leaves in her wake
 insisting on curing the sick
 by some unclear graft
 to bloodlines and nursery rhymes – passing

centuries of empty hands
to the deepening kin. Its turning measuring all –
even the shit unenterable,
this wielding of small nations . . .

I've seen as you have
how fires burst,
still-bred, laconic days cuffed
in our throats with the full range of lights
whose considered dimensions
still teeth the stars and forbid us raised fists.
A kindling darkness throttled
through berry-juiced veins

 this homo-colonic finish to an age
 of sinister divisions, cosmos black-spilling,

homo sap rusted through epidermis
after epidermis after frosty epidermis –

And even then we know that light-clung
horizon paused by its motley
ventriloquist is still foresight

That all the forests of Europe
have left their clutches
of disconsolate earth
and with afros flaming through centuries

 still walk
into the seas.

THROUGH THE FLAYING OF BACKS
after Ta-Nehisi Coates

If you know someone who'll turn
into a dark stairwell and rarely
be held guarded for having no
colony, no dues, no names
with meaning, here, bone-deep things
that escape chilling calls into the sun,

I am ageless and soft, fury reckoning
Western salt in Eastern wound.
Much like you, maybe, much like
opened glooms that trawl some meaning
from a violence of grief and best practice,
chief above our unpaved bodies, we
dare – our skins as uniform, a ceaseless
shame-end, a battle ranked for immunity,

retreating from your phantom whip, returning
with the creep of your fingers on the rod.
Unfold your own kin against these subjects
of playgrounds and stairwells,
these forty-second century lithe combats
with bone-deep legends, still darkened,
oath-bound to last names that can silence
the sirens. We too want the result of the unassuming
sky giving back its birth-water to the parched plane,

Something offered as a fissure in my throat –
I batter from plantation to plantation, again, these tracks
of tears again, that middle passage swings
on a periphery of dogs bound to posts or a rascal, rascal dark,

on through to a flaying of backs. Our frames at play,
hoarding all we expect to fail, under constellations
never named for us but in our own rivered voices.
Split this gaze, unlike who'll turn, rewritten and erased.

And what of this eager child that strangles as you
cloak again and answer to your own suffering?
Now, if you want your fancied truth
go where the tide comes in and goes out – I don't know

HERRINGBONE

You design in colour, that film that plays
in black and white but one false light
has riddled the projectionist, has paused
the aimless oracle exhumed in the risen credits
                    I am readied now –

With your mothers and your uncles,
your last wills and your brackish
testaments, I give me another hymn.
The unanswerable freedom
in this vast, unoriginal fear, I
do not come to join, the bleeding
                    though I must –

Split this wood: my claws, armoured against
this world, its way with woes and chanting flame,
some language destroyed, squared off
in the burnt prisons' prisms, these
generations of fear for which
of our figures might scuff and
                    be torched next –

Take my cause, my one true litany
of war, bylaws, codes and all
this evidence pinned to nowhere –

Give me pause when you cannot
find me apart from my laughter
and noise and the brutal language of my name
in your mouth, throw down all your man-made things
                    I am readied now –

ORIGIN OF THE BREACH

Did we long suspect the smokescreen
would lift the warring equilibrium's rapt
mathematics, hazards pinned
along a bruised meridian, everyplace abandoned,
everyplace to the amorphous ruins of Africa?

I sing its America, Caribbean, Canada.
I fable a European imago cut off from the burial
of its prolonged impulse. Who repairs this mise en scène of
coiled centuries, interludes and opalescence
        you congratulate
        in a still of sunlight as this skeptic drags
that entry sign still bound with bars and nets?

These centuries correct as intended,
where the elements of the world
brace no bars to execute, nautilus
this nakedness and prized psychosis of
bullets. No synonym for rape, blade, lynch,
disease and terror – everywhere there is
error obscured in added realms and
pathology as inheritance.

Why stand still at this edge where light
and her children employed in darkness
humour to cope with treats of dread,
alarm and mockery beyond October
sing us back, teach us shunned first policies
too close to smoke, screens and mad police.
Here villains still unmask scraps and rap
at assemblies for these children of the sun.

Who goes back to the incinerator, the dumped
prisons, the Seaview Baptist Church,
the ville laid in the dark, awake,
this fantastic lineup wrapped in the globe.
Man sacred man lined to the drapetomania surgical
clinic. Ti Jean, do you live for the coming
dusk, after all the burning talk?

GIVE BACK OUR CHILDREN

Born
with mouthfuls of ocean
give back our looted brains
our boys with shackles
at the scrotum, that manhood
famed for, sentient for DNA,
unaided. Earthquake models
of pissing whips. We need
no deep-cut postures
to support the weight
of plotted shadows, drifting
the wild quadrupeds
in our girls' starlit tears
still, fractured, refusing
to water our own
pillaged times

Our children are born
with mouthfuls of cotton
hands full of plantation
dirt. We need no deep
conversations about them,
dead, still hanging
like dried cassava, aplomb
free inside our quarky throats
while we're still walking
long, long miles charged
and singing, or morphed,
in immigrant schemata.
To be heard is, to exist is,
to exit virtual news-
worthiness. The voice, second
class turning heavy
at some remount of numbered
warrantees. Give back

our children, still
born indigo

with mouthfuls
with mouthfuls of blood
with mouthfuls of arc
with mouthfuls of dreams
with mouths full of cotton
with mouths full
with mouths
thank all the deities
for their
root-thick hearts
for the cosmic bulk
of their lips

FIRE OF ROSEAU

If not a note, a hole. If not an overture, a desecration.
- GWENDOLYN BROOKS, "BOY BREAKING GLASS"

On this ramshackle altar I spill all myself as k-oil, again and again.
Leave me wells of soldered mouths to climb in.

Or were I just echo in a slip of valley, empty room of black
mahogany. Together with twinge of sea and a lungful crawl
to the estuary,

I've lapped up all bioware before, all savage in the small incisions
of your skull,
all invisible shrapnel along blades of sugar cane, all peeled
from some benevolence in

your gazing centuries. Like the zordormé I speared with visions I regret
to think, while still here unbending, unending, that stranger
I've long stopped to frisk – only now

the jangling mothers have forgotten the brew. Who is still here to sing
junkanoo conch and still there suffocating – and would eucalyptus,
chandel môl and ash of sage do?

Forgive these unanswerable demands. Whose mouth with its own tongue
built this house in the thick jaws of this distance? Forgive this beached
animal between birth and

wisdom and you can question the only thing here still true – septet of my
exorcism, beyond my limp and brine, I am here. Igniting though open –
before

I rebel, I like any nigger with a demand: tell me my thoughts are jagged
but never why they bruise –

VILLAGE CRESCENDOS

Just because we're magic, doesn't mean we're not real.
– JESSE WILLIAMS, *BET AWARDS*

The long reach of this Massav Tree into the square is yours,

still in sight of the savannah. But even that is untrue:
we still scraping for bread in the after-bond of our flesh and age.
Not the way we both lived in a valley by the bay, penniless
as the spider looks. Not according to the Christ's coming. I don't yet

know what to mean besides looking out for better days,
besides rags for women named after terrain so hot
volcano bow in shame. But don't forget we laughed: how we learned
to boil the morning

sun from the woods of this mabouya, the intimate heat
bursting rum barrels all over town. How to remove our self
from the mirror – how just leaving here
with our blood unboiling was no way to pay our passage
into that cold Victorian country,
to no longer have to stand before that god of grief in thanksgiving
for food you wouldn't want to feed a fly. How toward everything
we're owed, we offer our reconstituted spine.
Who knows why the long reach of our canoes roll and return
that old Rasta drum to its cut cattle, the thing we can afford to ignore.

Repeat after me: give them a bad time.
That rapid-like vapour of the dry season turning
stone to bread, that still-Bob rocking steady its herbed gospel,
even now, as bookie bucktooth a will as I can tie to the boundary
of your chaffed lips. Still as you hold up that passion vine
your little son used to tame unruly goats, to bind me to
the unsettling of time in your gut, to make the years shadow
me like wheat transmutes grain: to be like rain,
wet with a decent happiness
to buff the scars that will not change me with your mouth

with river rock thrown mad on brown grass warning all
who think to enter and make ruse. What is today?
What calm period make them stories drift
in spite like the whole flow of mad rivers in this cropped island?

What collection of mothers we praise as they dip
their thumbs in the basin of each other's clavicles,
dab their foreheads with an oil as holy as their sweat
and nettle. You, gift my short heart some way to break –
Reach for me and let me feel myself be born
in that malady of troubles where bees still mark your throat.

So you sling back every letter on this half-burning page,
run its ash through time like metre through the line,
where shadows buss-up between
life and what short sound death make when it 'fraid.

Never there more desperate than anything
in a noose.

The impulse to drag your wretched arm out
from under that dome of burning bush and hallowed ground,
to spit out bittersweet root teas brewed for washing down
this life without sin,
this work of open windows,
splintered beds heat-bleached into practical jokes:

and you levy your anonymous coda against giving up,
against birth and plans for keeping alive –
by the heave of that same Massav branch,

OF ONE'S UNKNOWN BODY

One of these women stuck
on laugh, I, her blunting
chance to see a doctor who'll

advise like the blessed: imagine the English twang
is about making this decision: *who are you?*

Whose argons of lost literatures to keep
Whose arithmetic to set in the formula of
your bones. Except who signs herself
the zealot-way back to zero, a secondary glint down
a devising history, the black gold hills she's escaped –

Unforgiving as the grave,
science and metaphysics confuse –

the joke of who jumps out of which empire. Where is the hook?
And deprived, she can call the fall of any year so wished, familiar
with a whipping up, what lifts to hurricane.

She is only as true as the age man
spends between here and inventing another world,
another slant asking after the season
where the last five of her breaths rift

open the blackened page
and wander with the fisherman
who blights the sea after any ghost of her bones.

Our holy ones these salts have kept alive,
whose tales of keeping to water, maps of speechless centuries

names her boundaries, as she clasps shore after shore through my
combed peninsula.
There, the schoolhouse colour of some lunatic sea,
                    roiling for somebody

lapsed on some paragraph of stone. There lights
go off and reappear as cargo of waves,
fronds, fed up of the mind mimicking reprieve, there
in its moon-time pause for the children's indifferent scold.

There, clout or slave cutlass, cocooned seasons
in absinthe or a scissor bird's breach of reason.

ON BEING AT THE DAWN OF REMEMBRANCE

Who else of this wisped sea is
– tired of the ghost dance,
real, dreamlike too,

about the work of imagination,
an end by woe, illness, exit or post –
traumatic trees, uprooting

– not afraid to climb the fence
and leave a short sentence stuck
to the hands.

Give the post-prison child a break
for all the will and strength put up in ten fingers,
gripped on air, on any living thing, really: they who

entered 1866 and did not leave the same. Never mind these
yardsticks begging the untroubled ear nothing

but lovers' rock, country and western, jazz, blues
       And what's it to you:

who sleeps between the walls of this interrogation.

I do not come to join the bleeding, though
       I must

scale the walls of this brute semantic
off the unpainted wood midway on the boundary of the shantytown
       is rust even the just wind rejects –

So the grandmother still sits wide-legged
on a flat stone up the dogged path to her shack
       where all can bleed if she begs in a sordid tongue.

Bwilé, bwilé bwilé – she knows to sing, that burn,
a home in the exalted bay as night sways through entropic winds
pained enough to unburn the gummed holes in her clapboards
with stories about fingerprints tolling the superior man,

whose night is holed. Let it pass through us
many times more tossed than what we fail. I, woman

bloated with life. I, woman whose flood fogs the rite
of her coming, letting down what comfort I seek

I attend that sound she makes
that stuns
the laughing fowl.

SUITE FROM ISLAND 99

1.

She said: you know, 'nough things change
by the tall grass now living
where children once lay ball to pitch,
where the burnt coffee smell of brief rain
in hot, hollow savannah wood was a valley

still converting its occupants' welcome,
its mountains' pointed skulls,
this back-breaking life, its half-so-kind
its brief periods of grace

2.

and this sea that nothing here make sense
without, that this whole closeness of heat breaks,
leaping from the conquering skiff between them
pronged rocks where you score
your offers to the wind; but this
sound waking the nameless bones of all your
brothers; and the sealed heads of your sisters too
forgetting, it is not so hard to leave this place.

3.

You'll leave this old lady, she said, for that border
join up north-to-south, and become that creature-filling time
composing odes to the density of forests, long burned –
Is you. Is you: no? The mark in which memory feeds,
a stubborn feast of open seas and trite music.

When you can no more hear the birds,
than see your rank with a bottled script
flung from offing, washed up on drying heaps
of fisherman's net, forget
what is lost among them foregone saplings
that makes you glad, without weight of names.
You'll go and draw your name from the plot, from
time curled up in some agreement of homecomings –

Undead slaves at once denied their own bodies and yet trapped inside them - a soulless zombie.

MIKE MARIANI
"THE TRAGIC, FORGOTTEN HISTORY OF ZOMBIES"

LACKING THE WIND'S HIGHER REASONING

Propose this: if zombies slay each other on TV, redraw the atlases
deadbolt doors, faraway beds, small systems happened in the body
mid-chance reveal how thirst can carry the other in
toward remedy and bones as cutlery or the way the inner habituates the outer.

Faraway: atlases, doors and beds include our savage nature, though
closer to the mind's undertow, we've walked dead, feet-first from higher
    reasoning,
and've found prison street habitat for the good
we've tunnelled through to get here. With all of our grand books still here

we've settled for walking dead, really, to lock down the womb by calling it rib
– and that's not extinction, mind you, only music, that diurnal rage
humming the mouth. Sawdust spine, Scotch-taped heart
within signposts pointing the way to retake the composite scrolls home.

What persuades the zombie more than death hardly pauses a theory-in-slow-
    motion
so don't try. Or try the placation of shopping, malls, laundry, rooms, bakeries,
    hospice
forms for the acuity of shackles. But you're gonna need a bullet, a door, the
    atlas's
proof of the soul in its nighttime. Then proceed: make beds hard, keep backs
    frozen.

Try again once you've perused: shopping, laundry, bakeries, hospice.
Then, first: mend towards the sake of bones, their blueprint for cutlery,
and with bed-backs frozen, lift that shrivelled soul glutting the road, instead
proposing: zombies abstract that to slay is to scavenge the long-departed hand
    of god.

POLITE UNCERTAINTY
for Bianca Spence

Let me see you
leave with your
posture of stones.
Or pray, if you must, to your lit
from both ends artillery
where the world is reduced
to the height of your nose.
Best yet: is grazed on the boundary of your toes.

Your local memory, your pause,
cannot suddenly sag my syllables,
or whatever you trip upon outside
myself being invaded – but no –
Who reduced you to the work
of a tilted head, and respite, pardon my flare,
stretching the lips, polite?

But uncertain as what borrows now, as always, that dread
mock of beauty fusing mindlessly, the Morse code to the hieroglyph,
the telegraph to the Braille, the dying serif to the pixelated phrase –
throw in uproar the swallowed whole, the history as font.

Tell me how to be funny. Tell me how I haven't tried.
Lend me your gaze. Let me sign, stupidly, your name:

OPUS 23: EVE AFTER THE FALL

Sloped bark, night-breath, softening
the blackwood signs
in a city of words, wood and flesh,
water, a garden she could shepherd.
The Afrika Safari. What could you say
into May or June that could be enough?

The doppelgänger rib is not the secret.
There is always some reason to drop
the world off your shoulders, even
so that it can find its cry
            in the high horn of the lamb

Strike white lies about
the skull and wait
    for the mitosis continuum
of the honey locusts – all pink with icing
and revenge and soon
death goes shopping
at midnight, straight

through the gay, green heart of the tree
            of Eden that will be chasing
thereafter, the fire of Pompeii,
chasing – the white witch –

UP THE LIGHTHOUSE

Think you are apart from the name
      that stuck, apart from relics of
supersun, vulva and misnomer
   garden and virgin and beast.
   You must know, black isn't always the void:

to be a living fossil, light-years old
perhaps, the bougainvillea must think itself
aloof. That its fruitless state by twilight recalls
the bloom of suns. Small suns considered
suns because they remain, vibrant
no matter how barren the winter – how dark.

Think yourself manly as tiers of black pyramids
you mark, golden with vomit. Think the ancestral
footsteps in that spring-rushed courtyard, a stooled help.

Think yourself womanly as the one-eyed tower,
with patience to turn a thousand years of rancid
butter into a mountainscape
of nigger dreams, ascending –

black isn't always a void.

AND IF TODAY I DIE

for #TamirRice

I have not seen your death
not sung for the gathered.
      A girl can only do so much.

Words, the debt of figurines, pottery,
travel books, burned into this tongue
  begs Caliban your reason,
  begs Crusoe your doubt.
Gift them both your soul, an iron thing
still licorice and action figures, an empire's
return on investment.

None of these strangers who make
your name a trend, in the matrixed alleyways
of telemetry are the well-dressed men in
your nightmares, whose instruments
fuse you to the deafening sound you and your
mother rejected in the womb –

It is not your song that smalls the world,
not your pseudo-trigger that misses the world.
Is it the crowd of mothers and kids
who rained on the umbrellas
held above your bloodied self?
Or is it their shadows generations apart
that beg the watchmen show up and answer?

Each curious twilight of the listed dead
on streets, still gather to watch the passing light
as the votive pixels wait.

Maybe my mother will bow in her post
and caress the ground beneath this final weight and wait
  for me: I am not any boy with a toy-ode to
some amendment. I am a black boy – amen – who can feel the scour
of a coming exoneration the second I become
the faint smell of a worsening wound
sealed shut. Sing for me, alright?

SONS OF ORION

for Alton Sterling, Andrew Loku, Philando Castile, et al.

I wanna live, son. But which son are you?
   There where the rivers are made
of moonshine and the lights still wait,
    move by the music of the dealer's bootleg CDs.
Have you left the street-side, the Rigel stage
    for another watery home?
What still lingers by blood, the bulk of wound
        in your ghetto sonata? What bites the freak
off by its defiance of bandages? There may never have been

an autumn too sacred for this summer solstice.
   Given the body's exotic architecture,
it's prostrate before the cosmic rubble, its willingness
      to cope with joy as it spins
farther out from knowing too much of the bulk
   not enough of the blood – the creeping
catatonia passing for touch and air – on the studied shade
      of night bleached in a sunlit porous concrete.

   Who were you before? SOS. Sol. And if not the names
on this subsolar roll call: do not try to pull or remove your stitches on
your own.
      Whose Sol are you, then, *son?*

River Fort King Whisky Knight Mathematician?
   Sun like mountains turned
through co-op effort, black at night?
Sol still in declination? How far would you go

      to make sense of sunburn
    to make every candle yearn
      make brief light and pray how they taught you
        light and pray, too, this light is yours –

AT THE END OF THE WORLD
for Sandra Bland, Charleena Lyles, Darnesha Harris, et al.

       let fate choose for itself,
its patterns of proof,
– I hope, some child, undivided, will wave
a code through silence and a balance.

Unless seduced, hieratic, the ways
of fireplace or orchestra – kill still
– throw the last nutshell in for failure,
cast a troll of years remembering
itself, pushed through some unpalatable
darkside, exhausted, aside from ceasing to be human
       I found you in open road
       I found you all shredded
       If I tell you this makes me sad . . .

Who cares, for a snake clearing new skin
usually the subject of falling in love,
burning from a chained mask, cuffed,
bruised, even in the lone shadow of that inland
ruin, smiting us the carried song of another

monochrome Earth. Pseudo-seasons
ambushed in stasis, by starlight
splashed on a bleached form of tower
from which to leap into nothing
and hover, calling to be unnamed.

If you are not ready to string your
haunting touch against the breast
of some burning bush, lift no ash to
the dirt-black smoke across the field
for whose sake this scorned race,
ancient too, merges with the night,

stumbling still, drawn out in the solitude
of formulated virtue, one from another
for centuries in the seaward gaze of
the slave ship's bell, whose captains hum
and take more gold: *la vie sé un belle voyage.*

AN EMPIRE'S TAB

This news is a fingerless hand, pointing
to the field's script, always dark and vast
full and empty-like, where someone
else's smoke fails to orbit while
an empire and the telephone lines sag the same,
to be tossed by the hair, into the flames.

What we sought in our youth
never came from overseas.
This dying scent filling our hands
as the crows stood by and bled blue.
Still this isn't you, hardened
on altar and petri dish.

Yet to think of the yellow truck
rusting that old yard, yet
enclosed in another colony:
This impossible thing, the smalling of
many giants, a chicken perched on a throne,
making its Atlantic trip in a black canoe,
whom a sea of fireflies serenade, invisible from our ruin
       whose price was as human as any object –
       venerating its signature practice of wrath.

And by the monstrous star-dimmed waves
coursing through some other life like hushed rivers
of obsolescence, you reach for that old scripture
in the ear of your beloved and conjure dreams
for white Christmases, unspooled in that old logic
of anaesthetic leftovers, dead kings
resumed in their ancient posts, before
every word on *this page of sand*
falls to be sentenced,
far from your concreted place in the front yard.

This is how they left us. This is how to break
the night so that by morning
in another dimension
you will write me to say: here we are no prisons' bate,
no minorities
here, we know Lords
only by the scent of their tears –

TURN RIGHT AT THE DARKNESS
after Afua Cooper

Not a single could at summer's centre,
so vapours rise having run out of country,
of pavement to disappear in. Here,
this beginning season of straw hats: the basic bronze
of semi-nude tourists was like the dead, awaken

to walk through the wooden city blocks.
Montreal – what have you begun here?
Are these your Nouvelle-France remains
of an aboriginal dark? The place of here
that had died unfolding in creek, wood, totem?

But me. I am here for Marie-Joseph Angélique,
whose story pains still the boundaries of Old Montreal.
Not yet canonized with folk songs, with the metonymy
of air tornado'd in the throat: hear me full of the tragedy of her life,
the black rubber keeping silent the exploding atoms in the power lines

that here still bespeaks the province. What still forms
the northern edge of the St. Lawrence? Holy Notre-Dame
singled in the high-priced art. Rue Berri burning what axis
levels through Saint-Laurent. Saint-Paul, how you bow
even lower at the parallel run of Notre-Dame.
None of you
ever touching.

But what brave cold scars the maker of repair I seek,
whether witness or destroyer in the tested language
of sunlight forming in the permalink of the savage child,
the shaman's shaman yet, the brass of forgetting still here speaks:
     unbury your vex, oh, glossed maple flame
     in the amphetamine glass, the jaded plane,
     mimic of Oort clouds, still an interstellar show
of how radical the water under pressure.

Like I seek Angélique, amorphous, disguised,
quantum of that dead man's cool,
in the rogue geometries of a dumb gallows
talking plain the danger as though it were a simple dip
on a map. A place to turn right
at the darkness
between here and the master's room.

FIRE FOR THE GHOST DANCE

Somewhere, in the home country
a single birthday holds party guests
from the continents in a night-weep
in a singalong atoning
no real danger-song set
in the coming bonds. Ori have coloured

somewhere, the erratic contract
of this anti-story finding language
in spell-casts and sails and a sworn
dreadful love, a loss of everyone's
belongings, apart from these guests:
a refugee, a cripple,
a slave, a boy's-boy, a girl's-girl
            or what blows on the power lines:
            the aluminum
            in the rope tied to
            one helium balloon.

But none of them had seen
anything as red as this coral
Sunday. Skyward, heads strewn
by the round pool's swallowing
the dark-inked smoke of the fat wooded pit.
Falling back like everything
the valley forsakes: future economies of
            rock dust bed.

These embers against
the coming dusk-stroke,
the firing squad in every mist
of mangoed breath, recalled instead,
in the rye, the pinkish meats, cubed
and ground and painted by the tofu shadow
of dying clouds, the starting bonds
already hard until by night they root.

And sometimes the captive, unfettered
in the simple movement of a wrist –
remind of the towers, all of them,
fallen like us as we'd been left to deem
everything small, everything ours.

Somewhere, we are not just desperate blood
castled in skins, bound by visions
of what we once were, of knowing we love
what we hate, mirrorless and haloed
in ores of heavens greener than this.

TONIGHT, THE MAYFLY

The mayfly's elliptical
end looks like some ruined plan.
What's buried beneath
islands? Not the catacombs
of blended footprints
coalesced, and the entire
gathering of the missed who
wait at the prisons' gates.

If a kingdom ever spawns beneath my shifting
   skin, give me claim to another earth,
until all my confessions have fallen
like ghetto cobwebs, ebbed in

the wound of another excavation. The sacred
books of whose viscous clouts of invented ancestry,
I demand answers if only for the few hours I have left.

Inconvenient – I grow tired under the
artificial red of this flambeau night.

But whose letterheads grow tired of my ruse?
What actual figures fail
in the new stomachs you hope,
unaltered, will calm the seas
that make my selves unclear? I count the brittle
bones at the foundation of a family underhand –

In vas(in)deference, give me
any stake in a calling
higher than my double-visioned self.
I am yesterday, there, and then not –
   In a dream I hold savage,
   open to strike February into mullet
daughter, gestating son, miss teach,
choir girl never nun to a mother's discontent.

Some sonorous exfoliate in
our every feathered memorial for we are like mayfly subjugations
to what's still, a one-way glance through the window of some moving craft –

We do not suppose
Pompeii more tragic
than our invisible ports,
bearing all our children into
the potholed plan
of that inheritance.

So, tonight
between our teeth, between
index and thumb, between
washes of coral
and the immobile Achilles

these pronouns balance on middle
finger, this side of the chained meridian,
the brass that we dissect, the hereafter:
  commonwealth
        cistern from palm-woven basket
        Dracula from laja bless,
        René Descartes from Sesenne Descartes
        Irish moss from the grilled pigtail

Decline with us into the mauby valley, unearth your tune and reverse time.
Why choose sides when you've found the doctrine of sudden bloom.

Well, that strandy radio beep
kinks in the muddled script –
this time, choose not to hear
that ethnic name in dewlap misnomer,
  or colour codes to streak like hair.
We are not your fingertip calling wind –

into your own insatiate coffers, bate
by single-ounce ghetto youth outpaced on
city corners. Swapped for palladium stars pinned
to your chests. Who rigs these four-by-four
cyphers between their bars,
between charcoal and wall, who banks the coloured loot?

Looped tracks are these that pile up
in the trodden mines of the black mouth –
a minor place for the Mighty Sparrow's dying.
The day is brief where Tupac fumes the breeze with Beethoven.

These net worths sway through us brightest when telescopic.
Yarded and beating, like bars across the skull of the earth,
count on us to stay anchored, pound for pound,
a million small lives

with no irrational fear
of flashing lights
on the long way to the Cradle of Mayfly.
Hoards, what joy to outlive the fishflies

without ever loving the eponymous
music of the chain-link

    fence off
the ghetto.

GHETTO BIRD

     if infinity was a ghetto bird
     forewarning might have been the lamb barbed
        in flood alongside propane tanks / looped
  big bangs descending non-existent

 winds tearing brick from mortar while she slept

    you decide what more could she sculpt
out of nothing, or another kind of unthing:
     her lovely anti-storybook anatomy / the forceflood of man
     between her childhood effigies

the revelation too plain for any station of the cross

    come home, then, wave your white flags.
  What
     is war if not everything I risk in speaking here,
     too young to call it by name,
    like the blind imagines the shape of infinity's embrace pushed up
    against the black of her place at the edge, this abrupt collision
  is some secret
     screamed inside a penumbra

    already she is peeled back, revealed in opened parenthesis
her dreams are already overflowing with mud

  where empire still marks its slogan in her gone-father's palms
   where she may once have been the never-ending

she won't bother dreaming tonight: petrified grass already scars the path
between up and sleep, both tips pilgrimed with fools and she is among them
  but if she's big enough to brave the coming gush, sweeping brown through
white hibiscus like a paintbrush envisions an opening up, heaven pelting down again
  should she fall into the mud
  does she sink
    has she sank

FINAL PRAYER IN THE CATHEDRAL OF
THE IMMACULATE CONCEPTION I

Who sought the theatrics: Who begged diagnosis
get us off the hook, keep us in the rhapsody,
and what force infests the night out of cad ventriloquy,
the inimical boyhood that taunts us, the symmetry of shattered-strong

women, even still the ones with tattoos
of swallows growing up on the small of their backs
could all look loved in the right light, the painted light
       mything your glass windows.

What else is worse than nuclear fallout that I do not fear?
Tell me there is nothing mad in my foreign-smelling black
and I will mouth the dusk as it canopies
this sanctimonious debris anatomized in the mirror.
       Tell me and I may sign myself with your cross.

When without ever coming back to fix these battered wombs,
already forgotten or only glandular to what has been
I bargain for remnants of dreams like shards of ice in the eye.

There is no need for ancient landscapes now, no penance here
through televangelists, no grassquit slipping these vines to wine.

Peel back the scales of these untranslatable African songs, reveal
them more syllabled than your "Gloria." And see the black-toothed *Homo
habilis* you'd expect. See queens and knights left over to check-

mate. What is harder to deal with than an island nowhere with
       its catalytic lack of witness? The annulled
reek of bodies clustered for decades to keep from killing most things?

No one ever came to my door in searching –
for you, no one, except for you –

FINAL PRAYER IN THE CATHEDRAL OF
THE IMMACULATE CONCEPTION II

In the end
we'd settle on paraphrase

Tongues prostrate, still, like sages
after a lifetime of silence

With our names abandoned in
the weight of our diviners

Our serial practise of voice
the unthinking

deep within us,
crescendos through space

ornaments in place of moon
and air

everywhere,
coming like a dawn, withheld

bursting, we descend
with the countdown of our rebirth

with the return of early spring birds
littering the sky, we

water, hunting ourselves *through*
a rare falling

– are prepared to know our defence,
keeping it locked when we have no use for it

how, at first, coming home to crayon'd walls,
strokes of pure spirit and bone of the ones
who drew them, now absent, makes us

mad. What we ought to have heard
in the warring voices fleeing the night
as we carried on our fleeting fall –

was the half-rumoured lilt of thunder
in the baby's cry demanding plot
and reasons bigger than the guns
that stole us into a twilight we struggle
to understand.

– Ancient sages might have
spoken that same hyperkiller language
of dilating cervixes:

Labour is the early war, the one less feared
whose vaporous monotones of sorrow disappear too soon

And mothers – already overburdened by the fallout taxes of
some distant relative's original sin,
in which free will was enacted and land was spared
and bestowed by a God wise enough to
keep distance between earth and sky

– ask: who's duty now it is
to shed the need for things to come to blow?

That baldheaded anomaly in the
vulva's hoist

packing up its mallets, beating its sandals
one-handed, breaking tears as it enters the world

whose flaking skin is the utopist shade of the galaxy...

And who cares for these fables that console
but not enough

when the room half full of cobaltous children
when the age of the singing bowl
when the puppetry, fugues of string
and votive, withhold warmth only long
enough for us to clock our times

and return home. To the bad seeds
who've sucked up nicknames like
bandit and *colt* and *cockman,*
germinated from their toddling days
in company of small hulks and rubber giraffes
like secrets packed away in the attic

These are the children
we tell bedtime stories
of our undying
love
of the silhouettes.

So while we go on and limit sorrow to money and arms,
that knock-of-the-sill and conscience, blanking
the source of our ebbing genealogies,

our anthologized dead
still touch everything,

numbering the stars and known universe
as we find ourselves still prostrate beneath
a sun still raging, before any of us even break
into the work of our absence in the memorial,

we have been conquered,
fingers still jagged from battle,
and we go on
and we age
into nocturne.

THE HOUR OF ASCENDING

Back where that folked-out
full-lipped papier mâché hovered like ghost art
on this descent of solitude and its promise,

they came offering light, then backed away
from the mangrove in Roseau, leaving me

spiralled just so out of my outspoken names.
        Blunt forms of cosmology and physics:
church and *angel*, they say, but how to tell them
I am neither. Still, never mind that I have clung to both.

Recalling schedules of Sunday broadcasts,
deliberate formulas speaking cowboy, karate, Christ,
pushing me to agree with the seagulls' weep.

Did you know for whom they'd weep?
        Nothing returning of course,
        but the seagulls calling on and on,

in that galactic vinyl ringing on for light years.
Was it desperation that drove us mad?

        My ceaseless pilgrimage waking the sea when lights fail
        its depths, the long journey the hand
        must make towards self-portrait.

As if I'm still standing here in ghosted cane fields turning every age
        without ever breaking gaze.

Here souls riddle flame and song, they sing their terrible whine
        for me, these lifelong rewritings of self.

Keep your fables hearthside; I keep my lamplit door
        by one strike to the monstrous crotch of the Devil, his pitchfork
bent to a limber hunt for some new song.
See me – breathless in your airless pendulum
        – a Rambo-child who flies bamboo arrows into the depths.
        If only ever so to bear the beams of love, I am enough.

with fires turned to mountains in the sea
last children cuddled in the cold,
with hummingbirds cresting walls of volcanoes
with geese still breathless and astray
with the albatross humped down to seabed and core,
so the mermaids enact melodramas;
islands rocking gently
at the bottom of the Atlantic –

still, the lost children sprayed
unto New World, onto unbroken pitch, a country night
withheld, a whole unshone cantos of Papa Bwa

All of this while in the flaming, shed skins of the New West
takes to wind that still gust for every unwanted dream, afire
virulent times, our settling
ligatured to the boogaloo
to splintered crucifix, fish pot the canoe,
Hammurabi's judgments, the solvent
code of my gold-stamped diplomas

There I'm nobody, I's a whole blunt islet
from where you might deduce the dry season
from one mere cloudless day
from the sudden silence pushed into the bays
always home & algorithm of what history brings the seabirds

with whatever's still undiminished as the Black Madonna
if slipped so easily, that mellow Caribbean lilt
in Kanata: never think there's only us and the saltwater dead
aching louder than this worn-out world

as will be bottles still lodged in the sand, driftwood
emergencies of the many lost at sea who make
symphonies in these hissing waves,
as with looking back at the potholed woods,
where we'll be still, awake to speak, here, the love we know is there.
      Elemental fantasist dressed in black,
      here is your one, parched, ravaged world

Had they wanted then what they wanted now?

C.L.R. JAMES
BEYOND A BOUNDARY

THAT INSTRUMENT OF LAUGHTER

Nowadays I like to say *cool*
cool cool thrashing my tongue like iguana
before even a li'l wind ruffle my branch.

Because that was the dark, that was the dark
between my lips, saying nothing beyond the resolute,
so I forlorn, cool?

Here is where the chronicle of a small life
turned upside down, toward a heavy murmur
lets me make the place of my birth a fiction,
Kanata when I really mean Roseau.

Or calm, when the heavy hand really rests
there, casting its figure into flesh and heart,

I learned to be like the mute. But how to unlearn
contentment with silence within or without
that sorrow, never the same as the night,
though together they share the same start.

Wherever you happen to be
remember how the moon tilts its forehead on the bay
to permit the sun, erasure.

Here is where to picture the years
of seven and eleven means unlearning the multiplication tables

that I could only use in a black suit.
   They were many. They were few.

So I traded my calculator for a pencil, cool?
Drew icing all over the sky
Filled black gutters on white sheets
with fathers like lime losing seed all over the yard. Cool.

There I wished for a rope to pull myself out of the spaces
between sentences. Nowadays I can never be cool,
glad to lie on my back and summon no rain.

LET THE GODS TO DO THEIR WORK

A voice without calm as though half-dreamed,
you appear in scattered clicks of wind
through the low dry brush, where the world left you
lodged in a longing prolonged to grit
recalling: where the galaxy dims night is exile.
It was never a complex thing, the beginning. The tones of warmth
you returned with the constant remembering. As if nothing known enough
would shine for you a new-odoured air to carry your late-born promise,
remnants of sweet and singing mother. Twist of hand holding key,
redub of quiet, dust so dry fires conjure like atomic
supernovas until nothing lingers but my camouflage in
the forthcoming of my daughter, your daughter's daughter –
who'll do nothing but sleep for the first six months
of her life, re-watching: black glass engulfing lonely vowelled moons
while I ponder my evaporated heart

Lodged in a longing long turned to stone,
I talk sentences absent nouns and verbs
here, stone carvers sharpen your utensils with my tongue
and a shaking hope falls with a rain
but you never stilled what remained then:
designs to make you differ from the stars,
to keep you formless, shackled in sleep-wake, keepsakes
you'll never speak the gain: disembodied hands, a bit passage
I keep like a chill between my eyelids where something idles and night flees
until you fall out of blood and into water.
I'll always recognize you, keepsake.
Better than admit that we've lost
everything but the Christmas tree, better than
bear with me and your daughter's daughter, and habit so old it dares not weep

We have both of us landed now in the ruins
of a dusk so brave it waits for us at the door
lime-scented and liquored, empty like the washed-out pages of old phrase books
and us as we were born. Not free but eclipsed by our nakedness.
And what will be our banner as we leave our souls behind,
as our porcelain voices bend the telling,
as we release our names into laughter or breath flung upon the end of things,
as we give all of our indifference to the bays,
and I break apart in the only vowel we have begged
to exclude: that I, that dreadful *I*
tucked away in the woods as the mountains.
Was I there? Did I forget, pushed against saints and martyrs, the point of all this?

ELLIPTICAL NARRATIONS . . .

1.

The moment scribbles

2.

The morning after in its ephemeral abandonments

3.

The scale-like sense
        of an ending
curled to smoke
saving the world by loss

4.

If you will accept with accusation: oceans too must change
that their ancient forces of life may lift to hurricane

5.

This is no window finally opened, this is after-end
a stumbling to the river, to daguerreotypes
removed from the whole to be taught
    how writhes the root heaved from its maternal sand,
    repairs of a language over-read

6.

Stop at any point. They are never
rigid, those who watch
from the treetops

BRICOLAGE

Was I ever that young to come back now, like rain
Fingers the colour of blossom, plucking hibiscus from their mien
While at dusk the leisure star falls from altitude sickness

Valley voices sing and somnolent Gods weep protest
Where storm clouds complain but bring no comfort
Was I ever that young to come back now, like rain

Even when *the mango birds and children* vanish, the poet tells us
Of the common and good in our bones
While at dusk the leisure star falls from altitude sickness

In the happenstance of discontent and the mind
Grandmother storytells in flambeau with fireflies
Was I ever that young to come back now, like rain

For years to collect into resumés, orchards, tombstones
And treetops slump beneath their stubborn trail
Was I ever that young to come back now, like rain
While at dusk the leisure star falls and altitude remains

RESORTATIONS

Coming into harbour, cruise-shipped, indifferent
but for the graphed seduction of hills rolling into themselves

and where the sea licks that black Caribbean shore,
out of hurricane season
I see for the first time what they see:

everything the sea sings is untraceable
innumerable, this arithmetic of oblivion numbering my bones

or just protean, these encounters fall to summon
that same high praise: colonies of resorts along my spine

lay nothing on the back of poetry
which does its work in pH, in watercolour, in

whatever causes us to,
in some sense,
be cautious of time's dampening dusk

that every place of home must reckon malediction
even the happiness, which was mine – militant

like the dust in the schoolyard, which I've so missed,
as all words can be, felt, then lodged, then gone
using the gravity of the moon to rip holes into the self

I watch waves toss their comfort at the shore
And I still feel safe with my back to the hills,
that themselves will disappear like lovers,

like friends sometimes can. I strike a match and think
how lost I feel to watch the sun leave from the belly of the ship,
my faith in sunrise narrowed to the tip of my pen

LONG WRECKAGE

with mongrel's +/- children crusting
at the perimeter –
yet milk
cream, yet sugar

ferried into cracks by ants
surviving past a crisis of rhododendron
I watch the red beans of blue mountains drop into
shivering bags membraned with *diaphine*
one day to bite the children's gates shut

By the hour mountains of agrochemical bottles
announce themselves then turn to smoke
and what life exists beyond that roared wind?

Violet-coloured farm folk, models for national geographic
out working, tilling and ablating in high definition.
Such strange defence against sleeping maniacals –

Indivisible DDT from the lure of the brew.
Since they are safe in the dark
roast

in the maw of this abandoned government station
in Rodney Bay,
something stagnates.

I'm talking mule backs of burning contracts
back where Pigeon Point's elegant egrets phantom
freight ships chewed through
by ticked-off years rusting the humming sea.

Who is left to lull these Columbus lies? Calm me. Oh, England,
when the psychopathic winds that hauled
Africans out of address

have returned to song, to ocean, to verse like some
universe too far prolonged to cohabitate
nothing too sallied in our ground commonwealth tastes,
nothing more than parallels of things that I too whiten –

RIPTIDE BLUES
for Priscila Uppal

If I am to take the fly-leaf at its word,
know that I'm afraid this cosmic backstory will end
with no one to see me sob,
all my ounces lacquered to this steering wheel – you,
this doubt I drive down the marina, like words, sticks and cycles.

All mortal, a faith, infested, cannibal, as I read aloud your disputes
    put to rest along the string of Ulysses' bow
as the old woman's catwalk-dwelling cat across this
pond picks up the cellphone and reveals me to the authorities.
I am behind this wheel, unrestrained:
do let the sirens come. They will answer too.

Every unknowable thing unmoored
from the dead in your advice for burglars
in every tongue of the earth
what these tangs of ash must imagine
their futures plain, full mostly
of any living shard of the ones
they most beatified, least of all themselves.

What world is this that devours all
but the hauled-up vanity of dreams,
when the curtain lowers, with all four corners
pulled taught,
heavy, its centre a hanging belly
tempting genesis into the underworld.
Everything left would be open
to the criminals' logic,
like cinemas long emptied of ticket takers.

Armed with a megaphone on metropolitan corners, at the doors
of strip clubs, pyramids, temples and synagogues,
in pictures replayed aimlessly on billboard screens,
pixelated numerals running on thin sx strips,
in the pyscho-lights of discos and casino contraptions
someone will find me, mothered again by who
invites the burglars in.

I'll tell them, per your advice, to sit awhile and feast,
to get to know again our daguerreotypes'
methods of spectre reclaiming flesh,
or visions with returning purpose.

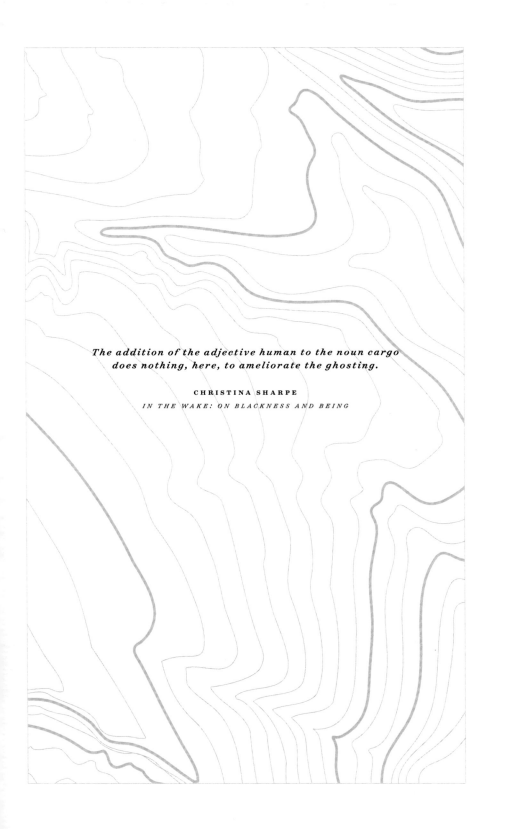

The addition of the adjective human to the noun cargo
does nothing, here, to ameliorate the ghosting.

CHRISTINA SHARPE
IN THE WAKE: ON BLACKNESS AND BEING

EPISTLE TO THE GHOST GATHERING

Dregs have formed us
molten inside. Here, a road, the core
this earth, a single-celled fire
a break in the vein: no exact archipelago
to dream what sealed its original shape.

Still we hail a fire that buzzes us in,
our swat-genes: still, our song
our burden beyond sanity: don't be afraid.
This may not have been the only home
reshaped by our before-selves –
Scarlet alphabets breaking the chains
of this age. Music not dialogued
in the cosmic blues.
A castoff in that short fuse, these
dogged admissions in asteroidal jazz.
Even loss can love what we mimic
in tanglewood, found summers in us –
A dance extinction loves, us until a great
height forms that almost-slay in us: come home.

Tell us what you know. Saturn
        apart from its moons,
        choice apart from slave:
        wealth before theft,
        birth apart from rapture of nation
        blackface scripted by lightning.

Mountains of your coast keeping watch for tsunamis
What fortune of helmets and bows form that one stubborn
fist close to the chest. Misshapen *O*. Pretext for a world
        whose dark children
collapse at the centre while the clouds in their radiance
call for night to keep on its shadow-play, a riddling on.

        Shapes of lives written in chalk, apparatus of black cats
filing this mirage of words on heroic horseback under: presence.
We wait for the bond to break –
What crossroads the locus, what zeal of Natives
sink my worry, my shame, perils still able to speak...
Mode of our entry into islands
Language of spirit sun, animal claw, dripped ink, post–stolen
            names.

Unsunk. Unworried. Unashamed. Unable
to speak the tenements back from their right
to realign the season's changing colours, maps
crested in the skeptic's eye –

From whose road do we now touch
all life that rains
the size and shape of dark becoming day –

Today I insist on the tenderness
I may soon forget and remind you

(of those memories: none of them mine)
there are no more telescopes on the pulpit,
no magnum for what we are: dark and lit out of sun
offshoots of the total
          frame that lights

You will remember,
the boreal plane.   You – not
a machine, not nation repaid with broken rocks.
Not torpor of countryside
          light takes a moral second to burn or has burned.
                    I was not always unbelieving.

What can we say of ten thousand years
Without the crushing levy of the soil
With the water of earth's first drop still in us
Mores of that creature taking names
Choosing to fight our urge for flight
Our brilliance indistinguishable from magic

If there is a science to explain our gathering

      it has not found me: it has not come for me.

If I have buried the sea in me, do not provoke

      the boil or the ground, unafraid, will break to remedy

this toil. Ask first whose probe has raised these rivers to scream:

ambassadors from Mars,

      oh, crypt

      of man

      all along

      extinct:

Was it in breaking
we found the symmetry of shrunken
heads in jars or in damp abandon, the fingertips
dug into rosaried shores? Whose blueprints enter
this wreckage of pearls unbloomed
from lightning between ancestral teeth,
from some sarcophagus of rainflies
we do not care to petition

smokeless fires and mothers' blès
all mere approach, all AWOL in frangipani,
indefinite edge of ocean –
       sweeping plain the water's edge.

       Before such vaster space:
       we reverse the bang –
law that loops on queue, life smaller than its reflection
watching the door, a dream played out in infinite turns of tarot cards,
impossible as their calling: citizen half-sunken in sacred mud.
       Now we watch for hours, fog fumble across its new
       expression. How true
the skeleton that frames the god.

Who is still in echo
                  as you, paused on a wordless
                        beach?
        metronome untamed –
            convalescence imagined in
                the dusk of things to come,
a childhood for a father-watch:
            I've already begged from
            its mute stoop
half because:
        who can not
        care for the girl-child
half because:
        what by a burning in
           your loins
                we know, still, to unsink

what was learned
from a life smaller than its repeat,

        that fragmentary gathering fixed in the stroke of a pen,
           in a boundless year's good bones

How these hollowed villages taught us to make our way
through hostile country, through mimic of first atoms,
a question: are we infinite because we are curved or curved
because we are finite
as the night we'd learn to unfurl from our skin
and roast turnovers on a brass banjo

We make such good roots of our dreamed earth –
We make soft the battle cry on our way
to harvest and bond. Is this redesign?
Does this not count a metamorphosis?
Resurrection at least, reincarnation or what's left of the bill.
What else is here to speak, what else but to take the partial roll call:

Australopithecus

Southern Ape

Homo rudolfensis　　　　　　　　　Man from Lake Rudolf

...　　　　　　　　　　　　　　　...

Homo erectus　　　　　　　　　　Upright Man of East Asia

　　　　　　　...

Homo neanderthalensis　　　　Man from the Neander Valley

...

Homo soloensis　　　　　　　　　　Man from the Solo Valley

Homo floresiensis　　　　　　　　Man from the Floro Valley

...　　　　　　...　　　　...

Homo denisova　　　　　　　　　Man from the Valley of Denisova

　　　　　...

Homo ergaster　　　　　　　　　　　Working Man

...　　　　　　　... ...　　... ...　　　　　　　...

Homo sapiens　　　　Wise Man

ACKNOWLEDGEMENTS

Higgs boson thanks to the editors of the following publications for publishing the following poems, some as earlier versions:

Room magazine: "Elliptical Narrations . . . ," "Resortations"

This Magazine: "Our Mapless Season"

The Puritan: "Aftershocks," "Tonight, the Mayfly," "Voodoo Hypothesis"

Forget Magazine: "Lacking the Wind's Higher Reasoning"

Contemporary Verse 2: "Bricolage"

Prairie Fire magazine: "Long Wreckage" (as "The May They Abandon")

The chapbook anthology *The City Series #3: Toronto*: "Ghetto Bird"

Arc Poetry Magazine: "Give Back Our Children"

Minola Review: "Opus 23: Even After the Fall," "On Being at the Dawn Of Remembrance"

The League of Canadian Poets' *News from the Feminist Caucus*: "The Mongrel," "The Stations of the Cross" (as "Pilgrim Dream: A Family Portrait")

To my editor, Paul Vermeersch, for editorial foresight and for lessons on the true magic of asking the right questions: I can offer no thanks enough. Utmost thanks to all the folks at Buckrider Books and Wolsak & Wynn, for championing this book, particularly to Noelle Allen and Ashley Hisson.

Dionne Brand, to whom I owe so much beyond language, and a thanks not yet invented: you are the ink of these pages. To Priscila Uppal, Jennifer Duncan and the late Rishma Dunlop for early encouragement. Thanks to Kilby Smith-McGregor for needed reading and questioning.

Thanks to friends, particularly to Rasiqra Revulva, and family – my lights through the dark; to all of you who showed up to my readings and gifted me things known and unknown.

Love to my mother, Anne; Maurice; Kaydene and Kaison for putting up with me while I wrote.

I'm grateful to my peers who inspire immeasurably. Thanks to those in the Guelph MFA poetry workshop who helped in the early shaping of some of these poems, especially to Liz Howard. To the poets whose words form the marrow of my pen: sea-wide thanks.

In your honour, cherished reader, I would find and name galaxies in thanks.

This book is dedicated to the displaced and in loving memory of my grandmother, Elizabeth "Matoorah" Edmund, who gifted me my earliest words.

NOTES

"VOODOO HYPOTHESIS"
This poem is after *Ultimate Mars Challenge*, a documentary that chronicles mankind's most ambitious attempt to find life in our galaxy through the Curiosity rover expedition to Mars.

"THE MONGREL"
This poem borrows words and phrases from *Death Valley* by Susan Perly. *Nèg maron*: Creole for maroon, or wild negro in the pejorative.

"AFTERSHOCKS"
This poem loosely borrows its theme and some words and phrases from Dionne Brand's novel *In Another Place, Not Here.*

"GIVE US FIRE OR THE BLACK PROMETHEUS"
Papa Bwa is a benevolent figure in St. Lucian folklore, who is the master of the forest.

"OUR MAPLESS SEASON"
The title of this poem is taken from Safiya Sinclair's "In Childhood, Certain Skies Refined My Seeing" from her collection *Cannibal.*

"CHILDREN OF THE ARCHIPELAGO"
Dwòl: Creole for *strange* (see French *drôle*).
Malfini: Creole for *chicken hawk* (named for its reputation as a chick snatcher).
Mizi maladi: Creole for literally *endless illness* (see French *maladie*).
Toutouni: literal and colloquial for *all naked* (see French *nudité*).

"THE STATIONS OF THE CROSS"
The line "by such strange cyclic chemistry" comes from Derek Walcott's poem "In A Green Night."

"FIRE OF ROSEAU"
Chandel Mòl: Creole for *soft candle,* which is the informal label for the wax candle mixture of paraffin, mineral oil and other ingredients used in bush medicine in the Caribbean.
Zordomé: Creole name for a freshwater fish.

"ON BEING AT THE DAWN OF REMEMBRANCE"
Bwilé: Creole for *to burn* (see French *brûler*).

"AT THE END OF THE WORLD"

The following lines are translated from Creole, an excerpt from the folk song "Si Mwèn Di'w Sa Fè Mwèn La'pen" ["If I tell You This Makes Me Sad"], by Sesenne Descartes:

> I found you in open road
> I found you all shredded
> If I tell you this makes me sad.

"FINAL PRAYER IN THE CATHEDRAL OF THE IMMACULATE CONCEPTION I"

The line "bodies clustered for decades to keep from killing most things" is adapted from a line in Christian Campbell's poetry collection "Running the Dusk."

"FINAL PRAYER IN THE CATHEDRAL OF THE IMMACULATE CONCEPTION II"

The lines "who cares for these fables that console / but not enough" is an adaptation of the line "The classics can console. But not Enough" from "Sea Grapes" by Derek Walcott.

"THE HOUR OF ASCENDING"

The last line of this poem borrows a phrase from William Blake's "The Little Black Boy."

"THAT INSTRUMENT OF LAUGHTER"

The final line is adapted from a line from Cara Condito's collection *Taste of Cherry*.

"BRICOLAGE"

The italicized phrase in the third stanza comes from Lorna Crozier's *Small Mechanics*.
Flambeau: a variant of the Creole *flambough*, meaning *oil lamp*.

"EPISTLE TO THE GHOST GALAXY"

This poem borrows ideas, phrases and words from Aime Césair's *Discourse on Colonialism*.
Blès: internal injury of the torso, usually the chest or back

The epigraph from "The Tragic, Forgotten History of Zombies" by Mike Mariani references voodoo bokor, which is pejoratively understood as black magic.

Canisia Lubrin is a writer who has published poetry, fiction, non-fiction and criticism in *Arc Poetry Magazine*, *Room Magazine*, *The Puritan*, the *Globe & Mail* and others. She serves on the editorial board of the Humber Literary Review and as an advisor to Open Book Ontario. Lubrin holds an MFA from the University of Guelph-Humber and teaches English at Humber College. She was born in St. Lucia and lives in Whitby, Ontario.